ON A MISSION: 21 SECRETS FOR COLLEGE SUCCESS

CHANTEL MORANT

ISBN: 978-0-9864165-0-7

ACKNOWLEDGEMENTS

The author of my life who has prepared the path for me deserves all of the glory for this book. My mommy who told me that education was my ticket to freedom inspired me to impact the world with my voice and story. Special acknowledgement to my brothers and sister who laughed at me when I was 2 years old as I read my first book without words. To my life partner who pushes me to be my very best, thank you for supporting me.

TABLE OF CONTENTS

Introduction

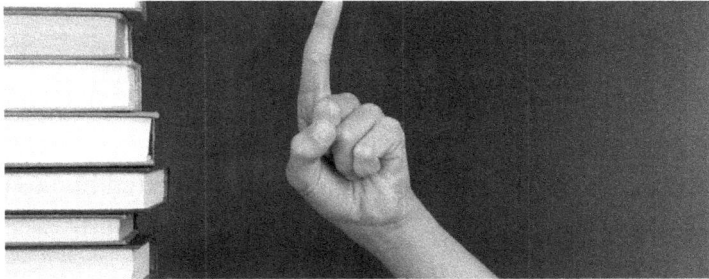

"The Best Project You Will Work on is YOU!"

—Coach Chantel

As I sit here writing this book I'm overwhelmed with ten-year old memories, memories from a time when I was just beginning my mission. I was eighteen years old. I had just graduated from high school and was ready for college, the next chapter in my life. Imagine my excitement when I got an email from the school of my dreams. I had been accepted into the freshman class for the upcoming school year—at my first choice! Life was good.

It took less than twenty-four hours for those feelings of excitement to transform into despair. Up until that point, getting accepted was the only thing that I had been thinking about—

money was the furthest thing from my mind. But when I got a letter the day after being accepted showing how much money I still needed to pay on my tuition, I panicked. I had no idea how I could come up with that kind of money.

Government aid and the few scholarships that I had managed to obtain would cover some of the expenses, but I had no choice but to take out a private loan. Signing on the dotted line to borrow $34,000 was the beginning of my life as an adult.

Time passed. Money issues faded at least into the background—and after all, I wouldn't have to worry about repayment for several years, right? College finally began. I was ready to embrace the next chapter of my life.

And I just knew college would be a piece of cake—just like high school. At first it was! Making friends has always been natural to me. I got involved in extracurricular activities as soon as I stepped foot on campus. I soon ran for student class president. I participated in special events and landed my first internship. Experiencing so much success so quickly made me think I had things figured out. I was wrong!

By the middle of my first semester, I finally realized I was badly over-extended. Clearly, I had underestimated the rigors and demands of the academic world. This was not at all like high school! I began to have doubts and anxieties about how well I was doing. I learned that college is not for the faint of heart. I learned that to be successful in college I would first need to do a better job of balancing my social life and my studies, to believe in myself, and to live off the expectation that things will eventually work out for the best. I learned not to sweat the small stuff.

This is the mindset that you need to have while in college. There will be plenty of moments where you will be uncertain about what's next. The anxiety and doubts that I have described were not unique to me but are normal for anyone beginning a new journey in life. This book is designed for you to uncover the secrets that have helped people just like you succeed in college. These strategies represent the combined wisdom of students who were academically successful, from students who were rewarded the most desirable and competitive scholarships and internships and from students who went on from college to become successful personally and professionally—and even pay back all those college loans!

I encourage you to apply these strategies in your own college life. You will find these strategies very practical in helping you achieve high grades, stand out from the competition and enjoy what should be among the best four years of your life.

This book is divided into three sections. The first focuses on your academic life, the second on your broader campus life and the third on your life after college. Although you should strive for balance in all things, you should give your academic life the greatest attention, particularly during your first couple of years. Be careful not to make the same mistake I made and get overextended socially during those years. As you polish your academic skills, do not hesitate to expand your horizons and activities. Keep your eye on the ball, however, and as much as possible think about how all your activities, academic and extracurricular, will contribute to your ultimate goals: a great job and a great life.

And please do not hesitate to contact me at my blog at www. RichBefore30.com if I can be of any personal help as you manage this next chapter in your life.

Your Academic Life

"In some parts of the world, students are going to school every day. It's their normal life. But in other parts of the world, we are starving for education. It's like a precious gift. It's like a diamond."

—Malala Yousafzai

Secret 1

Preparation

"If you fail to plan, you are planning to fail."
—Benjamin Franklin

How do you prepare to go to college? What should you be doing in the few, probably summer, months before you actually go off to school?

I would suggest you begin by going to your room at home. If people are home, let them know that you need to be alone and undisturbed for a half hour or so. Take a few deep breaths, close your eyes and just relax. When you are ready, imagine yourself sitting alone in a room like the one you expect to be living in at college. You have almost certainly visited the college of your choice and should have at least some idea of what your living situation will look like. Continue to relax as you imagine yourself in that place and time.

Now take an imaginary look around. What do you see? Are there pictures on the wall? Are they yours? What does your desk look like? Your dresser? Your closet? Your bed? Bed-spread? Pillows? Take a moment to explore all of the images in your mind.

Now, when you are ready, open your eyes and take a look around your room at home. What do you see around you that you saw in your room at college? What things do you see that you must take with you? Make a written list.

You have begun to make the transition from home to college.

The following suggestions may well have already occurred to you as you mentally explored these two rooms. Underline or highlight those that make sense to you and then get to work!

The first thing I would suggest you do is clean up the space you are currently living in. Imagine yourself returning home from college for Thanksgiving or Christmas. What would you like your room to look like? Like the chaos it may well be now or like a place that is clean and ready for your first visit home?

Above all, clean out your closet. Throw away or donate those clothes that you have outgrown—physically or emotionally. Think of your visit to your chosen college. You probably saw most of the students dressed casually, and you will certainly want to dress in a similar manner. But beware that even in this age of informality, there will be occasional events where you will want to be dressed more formally. Think about being invited to a reception for an important college guest or speaker. What will you be wearing?

The next thing to do is to make sure all the small stuff has been taken care of. Update your social media accounts. Get a physical check-up. Be sure money issues and credit cards, if any, are squared away. Your first few weeks at college will naturally be stressful. Don't make things worse by having to deal with stuff you should have taken care of in the weeks and months before you left for school.

Next to last, think about what your workspace or office area will look like at college. It is almost imperative that you have a laptop computer and an ink-jet printer (and don't forget all the power cords and surge protectors you'll need as well). I know, colleges all have computer labs and printers you can use, and if you cannot afford all that hardware, that will have to do, but making use of those resources can be a real hassle. It is far better to have that equipment available at your fingertips.

And speaking of your fingertips, you can touch type, can't you? No, not texting with your thumbs, but actually typing. If you can't, you absolutely must learn (and if you can type "sort of" you need to get better). There are all kinds of programs available on the Internet that can help you with your typing. It will be one of the most frequently used skills you will need in college.

Special tip: If you can, take a family vacation. Your departure to college marks a major transition, not just in your life, but in the life of your family. Commemorate that transition with the best family vacation ever.

Secret 2

Turn in Assignments on Time

"Life is the most exciting opportunity we have. But we have only one shot."

—Andrew Shue

You want to be known to your professors for good, not bad, things. You want to be outstanding (that is, stand out) for what you do properly, not for what you do, or don't do,

---

incorrectly. One of the quickest ways to get on the bad side of your professors is to habitually turn in your papers late.

Remember, many of your teachers are no more enthusiastic about reading your papers than you are about writing them. Don't make their lives even more difficult by constantly having them deal with late papers. Regardless of whether or not you are being asked to turn in your papers electronically or in hard copy, don't turn in your work late.

So, you have committed to getting your papers in on time. How do you go about doing that? Well, one strategy, if we can even call it that, is to pull an all-nighter and finish your paper minutes before it is due. Don't get into the habit of working this way! Not only will you not be doing your best work, but you will be placing yourself under unnecessary and excessive amounts of stress. You may kid yourself that you do your best work under pressure, but you really know that this excuse for procrastination is simply not true.

So what's a better way to go about getting your papers in on time? Simply create a false deadline for the paper. Set all your reminders, including an event on Facebook, for no later than three days before the paper is due. You can make this deadline even harder to ignore by agreeing with a classmate to exchange drafts by that artificially created deadline.

We'll talk more about your writing when we get to Secret Number Seven, but one of the sure-fire ways to improve your writing is to let your first or second draft cool off for a day or two before putting the final touches on what will become your final draft. By setting this arbitrary three-day deadline, you will be able to come back to that draft with fresh eyes, creating a final paper that you can be really proud of—and one that is likely to earn you at least a decent grade.

Special tip: Do not even think about plagiarizing your paper. Although there are numerous websites (and some classmates) that will tell you how to do this "safely," ignore them. In the long run the only person you are hurting is yourself. In the short run, because there are so many electronic ways your professors can check for plagiarism, you are risking serious trouble. Most professors will automatically fail a student caught plagiarizing and will almost always report that person to the college's disciplinary board, and that's a part of college life that you absolutely do not want to know about!

Secret 3

Go to Class

"80 percent of success is showing up!"

—Woody Allen

This "secret" seems to be almost self-evident, doesn't it? After all, that's supposedly the reason you are going to college (to gain lots of knowledge). Yet you will be surprised how many of your classmates are not able to manage the freedom college provides them. In high school it was nearly impossible to cut class. Either you needed to find some way of missing an entire day of school or you needed to know one or two fool-proof places to hide out for an hour or two (in my high school it was outside in the student parking lot). But even if you knew how to get away with cutting an occasional class, it did not take too long before your absence was noted (or somebody ratted you out) and the whole high school disciplinary machinery quickly kicked into high gear.

This is most definitely not the case in college. On any given day, no one but you cares if you go to class or not. Just as you

---

do not want to be known to your professors as someone who frequently turns in work late, you don't want to stand out by your absences.

Most colleges, of course, have established policies about how many classes you can cut before you end up on the Dean's "other" list. Professors, however, have the freedom of modifying those policies in any way they wish. I had one professor who made it very clear on the first day of class and on the syllabus (you have read the syllabus, haven't you?) that the limit for absences in his class was four. We were told in no uncertain terms that if we were about to be absent for a fifth time not to bother coming back to class because we would be automatically receiving an "F" for the course.

Someone in the class had the courage to ask if he meant "unexcused" absences, rather than just simple absences. His answer was firmly in the negative. His position was that if a student needs to miss more than four classes, even for medical reasons, that student needs to reconsider broader life issues and decide whether or not to continue on with that class—or even with college. Maybe those excessive absences, he suggested, indicated that this was a time to drop the class (or even college entirely), regroup, and begin again at a time when the student was in better shape—emotionally, financially, or physically—to benefit from classes.

So of course you don't want to be absent from class with any regularity. But on a day-to-day basis, what can you do to ensure that you will make it to class? I believe that the single most important thing you can do is to take control of your schedule. You naturally will not be able to do this with every class. You have to take a certain class at a certain time. Particularly in smaller colleges, only one section of that class is being offered. You have no choice but to take that class at the scheduled time. But in many larger colleges and universities, you may have your choice of different sections of the same class, and thus some freedom in building your schedule.

The way to do this takes a bit of self-analysis. When are you at your best? For many people this is in the morning, but others work best in the afternoons or even in the evenings. To the extent that you can, schedule your classes during the times when you are at your best. In this way you will be most alert, most focused and most able to benefit from your classroom experience. If the class requires active participation and discussion, you will be more engaged than your sleepier peers. If the class requires extensive note taking, you will be more effective than your less attentive peers.

Two final points about building your schedule. If you can, avoid what I call "aces and spaces." The worst possible schedule I can imagine is having your first class from eight to nine, your second from eleven to twelve, and your third from three to four. Those brief one or two hours between classes are too short to do any concentrated or extensive studying, but do lend themselves to another trip to the student union and a bit of socializing. You have shot your entire day, from eight in the morning to four in the afternoon, and have done little more than attend three hours of classes.

Second, do not ignore the possibility of evening classes. Many larger schools, particularly those in large urban areas, will have evening courses. These classes often meet less frequently and for longer periods of time than classes during the day and have a more interesting mix of students than day classes. Evening classes are an excellent way of utilizing time that many students waste in socializing, partying, or just "hanging out."

OK, so you have taken advantages of some of these suggestions, but you still find yourself stuck with an eight o'clock class that you don't really like all that much. What can you do to be sure you make it to class, in body if not in mind?

Taking a shower at night may save thirty minutes in the morning, giving you time for a little more sleep. On the other hand, taking a shower in the morning may get your blood flowing.

Create an aromatic alarm clock by setting your coffee pot to automatically brew at a certain time. Aromatic fragrances are known to stimulate and awaken your brain.

Disable the snooze button on your alarm clock. Snoozing is just fooling your mind into thinking you have more time. When you do this, your body relaxes into a sleepy state and is confused and haggard when the alarm goes off again ten minutes later. Avoid this at all cost or else you will awake feeling more groggy than you would otherwise. And put your alarm clock somewhere in the room where neither you nor your roommate can reach it without getting out of bed.

Drink plenty of water right before bedtime so you will have to get up in the morning anyway.

But perhaps the most effective way to get to those early morning classes is the old buddy system. Make a standing agreement to meet with a classmate fifteen minutes before class. Ask your friend to give you a call when he or she awakes. The chances of your breaking a commitment to a friend is slim and may well be that extra motivation you need to get to class on time.

Special tip: All colleges have a "drop dead" date, a date before which you can drop a course without penalty. After that date, if you (with or without the help of one of your professors) drop a class, you will receive an "F," no questions asked. That date will be noted in your college catalogue and website. Be aware of that date, particularly if you are having difficulty with a particular class.

Secret 4

Develop Good Study Habits

"The noblest exercise of the mind within doors, and most befitting a person of quality, is study."

—William Ramsay

You have been hearing about study habits since at least middle school. And since you successfully graduated from high school, your study habits must be all right, right? Well, maybe. But even if you did well in high school, college is a completely different deal. No longer are you going to classes five days a week. No longer are you going to the same class five days a week. No longer are you getting nice, neat, short homework assignments, which you will submit the next day. College simply doesn't work like that.

The first thing you need to understand about studying in college is the amount of study time that will be demanded of you. In high school, you had maybe one study hall a day and at worse two or three of hours of homework each night. Most of your high school time was spent in class.

This situation is totally reversed in college. To be successful in college you will be spending most of your time studying and relatively little time in class. The standard guideline for most college classes is that you will are expected to spend *at least* two hours studying outside of class for every hour you spend in class. The course load you can expect will of course vary from college to college, but let's say, for example, you are on a semester system and are taking five three-credit-hour classes, none of which involve any laboratory time. This means that you will be spending fifteen hours in class a week but, will be expected to spend *a minimum* of thirty hours studying outside of class. That means that your total time investment for a given week will be *a minimum* of forty-five hours a week.

Sounds like a full-time job, doesn't it? Well, it absolutely is, and unless you approach college with this mindset, you are wasting your time and money. Think of the sacrifices your parents may well be experiencing to send you to college. Think of all those student loans. Do you really want to spend your time in college sliding through with as little effort as possible? If that's the case, maybe you should drop out for a while, spend a little time in the real world, and come back to college when you are better prepared to benefit from this opportunity.

So the following suggestions for studying in college should be obvious. Study every day if possible and if your class schedule allows or at least study on a regular schedule. If most of your classes are on Monday, Wednesday and Friday, plan on devoting all of Tuesday and Thursday and either Saturday or Sunday to studying. Find a quiet place to study where you will be free of interruptions and distractions. Going to the library will often be your best option, while trying to study in the dorm is often a very bad idea. If you are a social person, study groups can often be helpful, but too often these groups are not very efficient and waste more time socializing than studying.

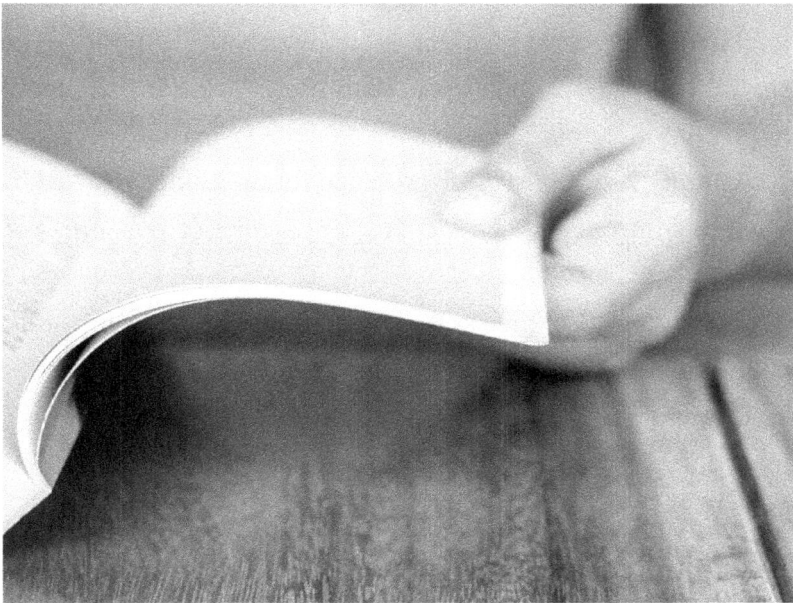

One final point about studying in college: be prepared for a dramatic drop in the amount of feedback you will receive as to

---

how well you are doing. In high school, feedback on your academic performance was almost constant. Between daily homework assignments, pop quizzes, formal tests, and frequent report cards, it was almost impossible to not know how well you were doing. In college, this is often not the case, and you should expect to go weeks without any sense of how well you are doing, and if you care about your academic performance, this can be a cause of great anxiety. In a traditional liberal arts class, your entire grade may be based on a mid-term exam, a final exam and one or two papers. You may have been going to class for a month or more, doing everything you think you should be doing, and have no idea where you stand academically. Although this is not true for all classes, particularly at the community college level, be prepared for the anxiety caused by relatively infrequent feedback on your academic performance.

Special tip: If the course you are taking requires extensive note taking, it can often be valuable to type out those notes as the first step in a study session devoted specifically to that course. In so doing, you are reviewing the class, preparing to continue your study of that topic and, of course, it makes studying for exams that much easier.

Secret 5

Meet with Your Professors and Academic Advisor.

"No matter how good teaching may be, each student must take the responsibility for his [or her] own education."

—John Carolus

I once had a professor who jokingly remarked that he believed most students thought that between classes faculty went to the library attic and hung upside down like bats until the next class. His point, of course, was that faculty, like students, have lives outside of class. One way of experiencing your professors as real people and not as creatures of the dark who magically appear at the beginning of each class and disappear as magically once class is over, is to make a point of visiting them from time to time during their posted office hours.

Most faculty members are delighted to get to know their students personally, and using this secret can help you in a multitude of ways. Your visit will ensure that your teacher will be able to put a name to your face. You are no longer just a name on a class list, a paper or an exam. Your professor will begin to see you as a serious student, as someone who is actually interested in the class material. Since too many instructors get visits only from students who are in danger of failing, you will stand out as someone who is different from the rest.

Be careful, however, not to overdo this strategy. If you are constantly dropping in on your professors you risk becoming a nuisance, which is not what you want. You should have a clear and legitimate reason for taking up your instructor's time and office hours. Make a list of questions or topics you want to discuss. If you honestly didn't understand something in the reading or lecture, make a point to talk that confusion over with your instructor. If you have a paper coming up in the next couple of weeks, talk through your ideas or approach with your professor. If you have an exam coming up and are not sure what the major issues or ideas are that you should be focusing on, by all means meet with your instructor.

Your relationship with your academic advisor will be different than your relationship with your professors. When talking with your instructors, you will be focusing primarily on the academic content of the class. When talking with your advisor, you will be talking about yourself, about your academic and even personal dreams and hopes. Of course, part of the time your advisor will simply be guiding you into courses you need to take, in light of your academic goals. But of greater long-term consequence will be the academic and career support your advisor can provide you, so let that person get to know who you really are.

These suggestions will become even more valuable when you finally settle on a major. At the beginning of your academic career, you may be assigned an advisor based on your tentative indication of a major, but the first year or so of college should be a time of exploration. When you do, however, make a firm commitment to a specific major, you will be assigned an advisor in that academic area. This person can be one of the most important individuals in your entire college career. Even if you never take a class from this professor (which is probably not likely), he or she can provide you with crucial academic and career advice. And when it comes to getting letters of recommendation, a letter from this person will be essential. Develop relationships with all of your professors, but take great care to develop an appropriately personal relationship with this individual.

Special tip: As a general rule of thumb, I would suggest talking with any individual professor at least a couple of times during a semester, but probably no more than three or four. Be a serious and engaged student, not a pest.

Secret 6

Get Organized

"For every minute spent organizing, an hour is earned."
—Anonymous

Remember those forty-five hours I talked about under developing good study habits which you should be spending *at a minimum* on your academic work? Well, by getting organized you can make the thirty or so hours you will be spending out of class as productive and as effective as possible. If you are not organized, those thirty hours will either be spent unproductively or you will need to spend thirty-five or even forty to accomplish what you could have accomplished in less time had you been more organized. You absolutely must learn to work smarter, not harder.

So, how should you go about getting organized?

Begin by taking an online time management course. Numerous courses are available on YouTube, some free, some for which you have to pay. The best free course I have been able to find is presented by StudentSuccessOffice (search for it on YouTube). The introductory video is titled "Do you want to change?" and is then followed by a series of short videos labeled "Strategy 01-Getting to know you," "Strategy 02-Organizing your time," and so forth.

The following suggestions are intended to supplement the ideas found in those videos.

Do not use those spiral notebooks, which you are more than familiar with from high school. Those notebooks give you absolutely no flexibility or way to organize or reorganize your notes. Instead, use only three-ring notebooks. You should start out each term using only one notebook for all your classes, simply dividing it into sections for each class. If you find that one or two classes are beginning to take up more space than you would like, then devote a separate notebook exclusively to those classes as needed.

By using a three-ring notebook rather than a spiral binder you will be able to add new items, rearrange items, and so forth. Set a goal for yourself that absolutely every piece of paper that you or your professor generate related to that individual class should be in the appropriate notebook. And by the way, the very first item in each section, or each separate notebook, should be the class syllabus.

Next, get yourself a date book organizer. Do not depend on a wall calendar, a desktop blotter calendar or your smartphone to manage your schedule. Go down to the bookstore, or visit a Staples or Office Depot, and find a date book organizer that you are comfortable with. Although there are many such organizers on the market, the ones I most often recommend are Day Timer's "Month at a Glance" or "Week at a Glance" versions. Whatever organizer you select, however, it must meet four criteria: first, it must provide a month at a glance function. Second, it must provide a week at a glance function. Third, it must have a place for a daily task list. And finally, it must have a place for notes.

Once you have your date book organizer, and once you have begun to work out your own system for using it, there are three essentials that you must commit to in order to make the planner work for you.

First, you must spend five to ten minutes a month using the month at a glance function to plan the next 28-31 days. What does each week look like? Are there any important dates or events out there on the timeline that you need to begin taking care of sometime soon? Use that five to ten minutes to get your month organized.

Second, you must spend five to ten minutes a day planning your day. The whole key to effective time management is to be proactive. Of course, some of your time will be committed to classes and other activities, but much of your time will be under your control. Plan how best to use the discretionary time you will have available for each day. And on the basis of that planning, don't forget to make a daily task list with the highest priorities highlighted.

And finally, you must have your date book organizer with you at all times because you never know when your plans will change or you will receive new information that you will want to enter into your calendar.

Special tip: Being organized takes discipline, but only through being organized can you make the best use of the time that is available to you.

Secret 7

Work on your Writing

"We are all apprentices in a craft where no one ever becomes a master."

—Ernest Hemingway

Writing—any kind of writing—can sometimes seem an impossible task. But for first-time college students, the challenge of writing at a college level can be simply overwhelming. The demands placed on students in high school for effective writing vary from class to class and are too often minimal. By and large, high school teachers themselves have not been trained in the demands and requirements of college-level academic writing, and few of them have published their own work in peer-reviewed journals. Even fewer have written books of their own. So it is no wonder that so many first-time college students face the prospect of college-level writing with uncertain skills and even greater apprehension. If you learned to write well in high school, consider yourself one of the lucky few.

As you think about writing in college, do not think simply in terms of one or two required writing classes that you need to get out of the way and then forget. Writing is one of the skills that you will use to a greater or lesser degree in most of your classes. Perhaps even more importantly, it is a skill that may well have a long-term impact on your success after college. Writing is a skill and a craft that, although never mastered, must be constantly practiced.

Aside from doing your absolute best in the one or two writing classes you will probably be required to take, there are three things you can do throughout all four years of college that can help you with your writing.

First, go on Amazon.com and get a copy of *Writing Skills: Success in 20 Minutes a Day* by Learning Express. This workbook covers a wide range of writing issues, which you should have learned in high school, but probably did not. Use this book not just as a workbook to improve your writing skills, but as a useful reference to correct English. Nothing can sink an otherwise strong college paper quicker than constant errors in punctuation, grammar and usage.

Second, take all the writing classes you can, even if they are not required. Most colleges offer not just the required one or two writing classes, but also advanced classes on writing and research. Regardless of your major, these advanced writing skills can be a crucial part of your academic success.

Third, every time you have an important writing assignment due, not just in your English classes, but in all your courses, take a draft of that assignment (typed and double-spaced) to your college writing center. Almost all colleges and universities provide one-on-one tutoring in a variety of subjects, including writing. Even if you are a fairly strong writer, the kind of one-on-one help and feedback you can get from a college writing professional can be exactly the help you may need to become not just a strong writer, but a writer of excellence.

Special tip: If you haven't learned it by now, do not rely on your word processor's spell and grammar check function. Your spell checker is just as happy weather or not you use it. (Did you notice in the previous sentence that "weather" is not correct? My spell checker didn't!)

Secret 8

Pursue your Passion

"If you can't stop thinking about it, don't stop working on it."

—Anonymous

You will spend more of your adult life working than you will spend in any other activity. You will spend more time at work than you will with your family and friends. You will spend more time at work than you will in all of your recreational time put together. Yet study after study shows that significant numbers of people do not like (and some even hate) their jobs and, if given the chance, would choose some other line of work. The personal and academic decisions you will make during your four years of college will have a profound impact on the rest of your life.

For our generation, work is expected to be not just a way of paying the bills but as a way of finding meaning in life. Yet often beginning in college far too many men and women have failed—or refused—to lead a life of meaning and productivity, and even more have failed to follow what the great mythologist Joseph Campbell calls "following your bliss."

To prepare for a life of meaningful work—which after all is what college is supposed to be about—you need to understand two things about career development. First, career choice is a function of personality and, second, career success is a function of the match that exists between who you are as a person and the requirements of your job. In other words, the closer the match between who you are as a person and the demands placed on you by your work, the more you will find your work to be a source of meaning and significance. The choices you will make in college and the courage you will need to demonstrate in pursuing your passions will by and large determine your success in life.

So, how do you go about following "your bliss?" There are as many ways of doing this as there are ways of knowing yourself, but I want to suggest one in particular. Go to your career-counseling center and ask that they provide you with the means of taking the "Strong Interest Inventory." (You should have taken this in high school but, with budget cuts, far too many schools provide only a bare minimum of career support—if that.) This inventory is the standard instrument for clarifying the link between personal interests and career goals. Use the results of the inventory to re-examine what you are doing in college, what courses you are taking, and where you want your life to go.

If your counseling center is unable or unwilling to provide you with the chance to take this inventory (which is not free and which must be computer scored by its publisher), get in touch with me and I'll provide you with the help you may need to get access to that instrument.

Once you have a systematic picture of the link between your personal interests and your career possibilities, ask yourself if your current or prospective major is in line with that picture. Don't hesitate to explore another major by taking an introductory course in that area. If you notice that you dread going to classes in your current major, think about what other classes you might want to explore. Don't change your major, however, just on a whim. Talk to your professors. Talk to the people in your college's career counseling center. Talk to juniors or seniors about what a major in a given area is really all about. Gather all of the information you can before making any decision about your major.

Special Tip: This is a major decision (pun intended) so approach it carefully.

Secret 9

Take Risks

"The biggest failure you can have in life is making the mistake of never trying at all."

—Anonymous

Please understand that going to college is itself a major risk. You are risking at least four years of your life, thousands of dollars and, most importantly, your future. Isn't that enough of a risk? Why should you even consider any more risks? Why not play it safe, commit to a major that you may really not like all that much, but that will at least get you a job (you hope) after college, and get on with your life? Any further risk-taking is just nuts, right?

If thinking about taking more risks than you already are keeps you awake at night, think about risks as nothing more that experimentation. This is the one time in life when you can take reasonable risks without, hopefully, suffering any long-term negative consequences. Experimenting with drugs is of course, a really bad idea, but taking an apparently interesting course outside your major may be a really good one. Try out a few new things; this may be the one time in life where you will have the freedom to do so.

Depending on your major, the courses you are required to take (and in what order) may be fairly well laid out for you. You nevertheless will have at least a few electives each year where you can explore interests outside your major. One elective that you really should consider that may sound way too risky for you is a course in public speaking. According to the *Wall Street Journal*, fear of public speaking is the number one fear in this country, ranking just ahead the number two fear, death. Just imagine, most people are more afraid of speaking in public than they are of dying! (The reason for this ranking of course is that dying is something that is well down the road for most of us, but I've got to deliver that darn speech next week!) Take the risk of confronting that fear while still in college instead of waiting until your job requires it of you, only to find that you are not prepared.

The other area of your college life where risk taking may be called for is during your summer vacations. I'll talk more about internships later in this book, but for now think of how you might go about expanding your personal or professional horizons during the time you are away from college.

Special tip: If the idea of taking significant risks is of real emotional concern for you, get a copy of Margie Warrell's *Stop Playing Safe* (or any one of a number of other books on Amazon.com on the topic of risk taking.) The help these books can provide may be of real value for someone for whom the fear of risk is a major emotional issue.

Secret 10

Use Free Resources

"The best things in life are free."

—Lew Brown

Just to show that I am not playing favorites in the following exercise, I am simply choosing the two top ranked college football teams on the day I am writing this.

So, first go on the homepage of the University of Alabama at www.ua.edu. At the top of that page, select "Life at UA," then take a moment to explore some of the resources available to students at the University of Alabama under the five headings you will find toward the bottom of that page.

Next, go through the same drill for the University of Oregon at www.uoregon.edu by exploring some of the resources available under the heading "Campus & Community."

After spending no more than five minutes or so exploring these two sites, go to the homepage of your current (or prospective) college or university. Find the link that corresponds to the ones you have been looking at for Alabama and Oregon. Although your school may well not be as large and as rich as these two institutions, the campus and local resources available to you will be similar in kind, if not in scope. Spend a half hour or so exploring these resources online. Almost all of them will be free.

I hope I have made my point. The free resources that are available to you at any major college or university are numerous and varied. Use them!

Special tip: There is one person on campus that you should make a special effort to get to know: the reference librarian. Wait until you are faced with your first research assignment, then drop by the library to talk with this person. Even in an age when all of the information in the world seems to be available online, you will be amazed at the unique kind of help this person can provide you.

Your Campus Life

No period of my life has been one of such unmixed happiness as the four years which have been spent within college walls.

—Horatio Alger

Secret 11

Manage your Money.

*"Beware of little expenses; a small leak will
sink a great ship."*

—Benjamin Franklin

The following story is absolutely true.

One of my friends in my first year of college, who had no experience with money management, had taken out a thousand dollar student loan at the beginning of the year for expenses, which he assumed would be sufficient for his entire freshman year. All of his other college costs had been taken care of in advance. He was on a full tuition scholarship and the bills for his room and board were going directly to his parents. So at the beginning of his freshman year he simply deposited the thousand dollars in a checking account in a local bank and proceeded to write checks.

Apparently, he never entered the amount of the checks he wrote in his checkbook and never even looked at the bank statements he received online every month.

I think you can see where this story is going. It was about a week and a half before the Christmas vacation that he got a call from a local supermarket that his last check had bounced. You can imagine the reception my friend received from the Dean of Student Services when he showed up a couple of days later asking for another loan. Somehow he did manage to get that loan but, at least for the time being, appeared to have learned a lesson about money management: he sent the check to his mom, who agreed to draw on that money, sending him an allowance every couple of weeks.

College can be stressful enough without adding money problems to the stress. Unless you are a spoiled child of wealth and privilege with a couple of gold or platinum credit cards in your pocket which your parents (or more probably their accountants) take care of every month—yes, there are such students!—you will need to learn to take better care of your money than my friend did.

Obviously, you need to work from a budget. Set up a checking account either at a local bank or at home. Regardless of where you set up that account, consider authorizing your parents to have access to that account in case of emergencies or accounting problems. Review the status of your budget at least monthly.

Borrow only what you need. It can be very tempting to accept all of the financial aid that you've been approved for, but remember that someday you will have to pay all that money back. Think about the difference between a credit card and a debit card. With a credit card you are borrowing money, often at a high rate of interest, while with a debit card you are using your own real money that you have deposited in that account. If you do want to get a credit card, get only one and pay it off regularly. In so doing, you will be establishing a solid credit rating, which will be of value once you graduate from college.

Explore ways of saving money on books, which of course are a major expense. I see no problem buying used, rather than new, books, but if you do be sure that the book has been only lightly used. Working with a book that has been heavily underlined or written in can be very distracting. And, of course, check out availability of new and used textbooks online, which can often be purchased for far less money than at the bookstore.

Special tip: Think carefully about taking on part-time, paid work while in college. If the money you would make in a part-time job is absolutely essential for you to stay in college, then go for it. But remember those forty to fifty hours you should be devoting to your academic life. Going to college should be your full-time job, and investing the time needed to maintain a high GPA will have significant pay-off after you graduate and begin looking for a job. If you can, keep your moneymaking to the summer.

Secret 12

Adopt Healthy Habits

"We are what we repeatedly do. Excellence therefore is not an act, but a habit."

—Aristotle

R esearch has shown a direct connection between academic performance and health. In a recent study conducted at Carleton University in Canada, researchers surveyed over one hundred college and university students and discovered that those who tended to put off their academic work until the last minute also tended to put off getting medical help when needed, failed to exercise, failed to eat a healthy diet, tended to abuse alcohol and drugs, and reported more stress than their more disciplined peers (see the work of the "Procrastination Research Group" at Carleton University, Ottawa, Canada).

It seems to me that the point of such studies is not that poor academic performance results in unhealthy behavior, but that poor habits seem to cluster together. So when you think about maintaining a healthy lifestyle in college, think about all aspects of your life on campus.

Obviously, you need to maintain a balanced diet. Just because you are away from home, avoid the temptation to eat anything you want. Avoid the phenomenon of the Freshman Fifteen, the tendency of many first-year students to put on that extra fifteen pounds. Eating excessively as a way to compensate for the stress of college can begin a negative cycle of sickness, lethargy and depression, which will in turn affect your academic work.

If you are at all athletic, get involved in college sports. If you are going to a Division I NCAA university, you may not be good enough to try out for the big time, but you still may be able to engage in intramural sports. If you are not all that athletic, maintain your physical conditioning by developing an exercise routine. Even small colleges should be able to provide the resources of a good health club. As always, the buddy system can work wonders. Commit to working out with a friend before or after class or on some other regular basis. If nothing else, go for a few long walks every week.

You should get medical and dental check-ups at least once a year. You may want to schedule these check-ups when you are home for vacations or during the summer, while at the same time filling any prescriptions you will need at school. If you cannot visit your home doctor or dentist, seek medical attention at a campus health facility, the cost of which is almost always covered as part of your student activity fees.

Most adults need at least 8 hours of sleep a night to function at peak performance. And if you are managing your time and your academic life properly, you should *never* be in a position where you need to pull an all-nighter.

Do your best to stay away from drugs and alcohol. College is a great time to explore new things, but keep alcohol and drugs off your "to do" list. Drinking and substance abuse are not cool for anyone on a serious mission to graduate. There are so many negative consequences related to the use of alcohol and drugs that it is wise to avoid them at all cost.

Special tip: If you do find that you are having problems maintaining a healthy lifestyle at college, seek help at the student health center. You are paying for this resource through your student fees, so you might as well use it.

Secret 13

Attend to Your Own Personal Growth

"An unexamined life is a life not worth living."

—Socrates

College is a period of great personal growth and development. Almost regardless of what you do, college will change you. You can, however, have some control over the nature and quality of that change. You have a choice: you can react to events as they come along or you can be proactive and take charge of your own personal growth and development. You can either bury yourself in the narrow demands of your academic major or you can take advantage of the incredible resources your college provides for personal growth.

So how do you do that? Simply use your electives to take courses that focus on the personal and interpersonal dimensions of life. Depending on how your school organizes its departments and areas of study, these courses will usually be found both in the Communications Department and the Psychology Department.

To show what I mean, I have more or less at random pulled down one of the college catalogues from my bookshelf. Here are some of the courses in that catalogue that I would see as potentially contributing to your personal growth. (Naturally you will not find exactly these same courses in your own college, but you'll get the idea.) In the Communication Department I find, among others, the following:

> *Interpersonal Communication*: Introduces communication in person-to-person interactions, emphasizing theoretical principles and their practical applications.

> *Team Communication and Leadership*: Emphasizes communication skills to participate in team settings. Covers the characteristics of small groups, leadership and conflict management skills.

> *Communication and Gender*: Examines the role of gender in communication and identifies many of the personal and public factors involved in communication between men and women.

And in the Psychology Department I find the following, among others:

> *Psychology of Human Relations*: Applies psychological principles to understanding relationships with ourselves and others.

> *Psychology of the Workplace*: Focuses on a number of important factors for effective performance in the workplace, including interpersonal skill development, conflict resolution skills, group problem solving and decision-making, and time management.

Think about how courses like these could help you understand and manage yourself better, while helping you build better relations with those around you. Then think about how these skills could be of value once you leave college. Numerous research studies of occupational success invariably show that the *single most important skill for success in the workplace* is what some researchers call "relationship management." You do not have to be a communications or psychology major to take advantage of the powerful ideas and skills taught in such courses.

Special tip: While in college, surround yourself with positive people. Birds of a feather do flock together, and peer influence

---

is very powerful in college. Surround yourself with positive, optimistic people if you want to become the positive, optimistic person who will be successful both in college and life.

Secret 14

Volunteer

"The best way to not feel hopeless is to get up and do something. Don't wait for good things to happen to you. If you go out and make some good things happen, you will fill the world with hope, you will fill yourself with hope."

—Barack Obama

College is of course about expanding your horizons, personally and academically. Volunteering is one of the most important ways to do this while in college and can have important long-term pay-offs.

In general, there are two ways of gaining experience as a volunteer. First, some academic programs have a service component in which students are expected to have some volunteer experience in a particular field, and this requirement often carries academic credit. This service requirement is particularly common in majors that have a direct, real world application, like nursing, physical therapy, hotel management and so forth. If you are currently in such a program, you probably already know about that requirement. If you are still selecting your major, and you like the idea of earning college credit for volunteering, talk to your academic advisor.

The second kind of volunteer opportunity does not involve academic credit, but does get you involved in activities outside the classroom. To find out more about such opportunities, talk to the people in your student services office, who will have a list of available local needs.

You can also find out much more about volunteering on the internet. Studenttravel.about.com can provide you with a detailed "List of Volunteer Organizations for College Students."

One of the many options provided on that site is Volunteer-match.org, which will match you with local volunteer opportunities.

There are many advantages to be gained by volunteering. Obviously, being able to point to such experiences on your resume can be of real value. You are showing a prospective employer that you can manage your academic time well and also have time to volunteer ("A 3.8 GPA *and* a volunteer! Wow!"). You are also showing that you have real world experience and that you have had the kind of experience working with different people that the academic world does not offer sometimes.

The second major advantage of volunteering is that it is a way of gaining experience in a particular field and of exploring your career options in that field. Volunteering as a nurse's aid is the most obvious example of this kind of benefit, but, particularly if your college is in a large urban area, there are many other businesses and industries that you would be able to explore through volunteering.

The third major advantage of volunteering is the personal growth that may well result as a consequence of that activity. I talked about personal growth in the last section, of course; besides taking courses in communications and psychology, volunteering is yet another way of developing yourself as a person during the important four years of your college education.

Special tip: As important as volunteering is, remember that your primary focus in college should be on academics, not on your extracurricular activities. If your resume shows a mere 2.1 GPA, being able to list tons of volunteer activities is going to do little to save you.

Secret 15

Decompress to Avoid Stress

"Inner peace gives you freedom to make your next move your best move."

—Coach Chantel

Sages and philosophers have been seeking inner peace since the beginning of time. But unless you are willing to spend a couple of years in a Tibetan monastery, you will need to find that peace in the real world of your college or university.

In a sense, you have already begun doing that. If you have followed the suggestions I have made so far, you have successfully prepared yourself for college, you are turning in your assignments on time, you are going to class, you are developing good study habits, you have gotten organized and you are managing your time well. You have already taken some of the most important steps you can to reduce stress.

There is still one more step that you can take to manage stress, and that is to set apart a special time for relaxation and decompression. There are numerous ways of doing this, of course, from listening to relaxing music to meditation. Even with the best time management and study skills, you will naturally experience some stress in college. Learn to recognize your own particular signs of stress and be aware of the kind of events and situations that cause you to feel stressful. Find the stress reduction strategy that works for you and actually schedule in time every week for focused relaxation and stress reduction.

Special tip: Two strategies I have found to reduce stress that work for me is to treat myself to a good meal at my favorite restaurant or to spend some time shopping. I have found that a little retail therapy handled responsibly is a nice way to lift my spirits. When I achieve a particular goal I celebrate in a small way with a small purchase. Well-deserved rewards are the best!

Secret 16

Find an Internship

"Be so good they can't ignore you."

—Steve Martin

An internship is a real, although temporary, job. Internships provide you with the opportunity to explore a particular career field, gain real world experience, begin developing the kind of network that may be crucial when you start looking for a full-time job and earn some money. Internships most often take place during the summer and summer internships are almost always full-time. You may however, discover internship opportunities during the school year. If so, you can intern, but I recommend only doing so if you are a sophomore, junior or senior.

In the past, internships were often unpaid, but the days of unpaid internships may well be numbered. Several recent court rulings, often in response to lawsuits brought by former interns, have begun to make it clear that unpaid internships are in violation of federal law and that employers are required to pay interns at least a minimum wage, even if the prospective intern has indicated a willingness to work for free.

In response to a Supreme Court ruling from the 1940s, the Department of Labor has laid out several criteria that must be met for an internship to be unpaid, including the stipulations that the work be an extension of the student's academic studies, that the internship be primarily for the educational benefit of the intern, and that the hiring company receive no significant benefit from the work of the intern.

Although these criteria are clear, many companies, particularly those in highly competitive fields, have continued to utilize unpaid interns. In considering a particular internship, therefore, you need to balance the experience you might gain from that position against the pay (or lack of) that comes with that position. I have found the experience gained from non-paid internships to be well worth the financial sacrifice.

For more information about paid and unpaid internships, go to richbefore30.com and do a search for an article entitled "Is the Unpaid Internship Worth it?"

The disappearance of the unpaid internship, while being good news for those who do manage to land a paying position, will inevitably result in the reduction of the number of available internships and increased competition for those that are. Because internships are therefore real, paying—though short-term— jobs, the search for an internship should be approached with all the seriousness of a real job search.

It can be argued, therefore, that one of the greatest benefits to be derived from searching for an internship is that it will give you real experience in looking for a real, post-college job. Even if you are unsuccessful in finding a summer internship, the actual job-hunting experience itself can be of great value.

Because of the competitive nature of summer internships, you should begin looking for your internship as early as possible and, just as in looking for a full-time job, you should apply for as many as are practical. Go to your student services center to see what they have available. Do a Google search for "college summer internships," the results of which will be essential in your search.

In applying for an internship you will almost certainly need to write a resume and a cover letter. Go online for successful examples of what these documents should look like. Don't worry if your resume looks a little "thin"; remember that your prospective employer knows that you are a college student and that you can not be expected to document extensive work experience.

If you get through the first round of the application process you will probably be invited for an interview. Go online for tips and suggestions about how to conduct yourself in a professional interview.

The search for an internship can be as difficult as any job search you will ever conduct, with all of the emotional ups and downs. Relish the experience and learn as much from it as you can, regardless of whether or not you actually do get the internship.

Special tip: Remember the communications courses I recommended under the personal growth secret? When you get to your first interview, you will be grateful that you followed that piece of advice.

Your Life After College

The purpose of life, after all, is to live it, to taste experience to the utmost, to reach out eagerly and without fear for newer and richer experiences.

—Eleanor Roosevelt

Secret 17

Make Post Graduation Plans

"The only thing worse than being blind is having sight, but no vision."

—Helen Keller

By the time you begin your junior year, you should have at least a general idea of where your life and career are heading, with perhaps several options or alternatives in mind. By the time you begin your senior year, those options should be narrowed down to no more than two or three.

For some, the next step after college will be clear. Land your dream job, drive the car of your dreams off into the sunset, right? Wrong. If it were that simple why would the unemployment rate be so high for recent graduates? The best way to ensure that you will succeed is to prepare for it. Interning as you know from the previous secret, is a great way to increase your career possibilities. Depending on how well you perform, your employer will offer you a position upon graduating. This is the ideal situation, of course. In the event you do not receive a formal offer, but know you performed exceptionally well during your internship, consider speaking with your boss to express your interest in working with the company. They will appreciate your desire and likely put you at the top of their candidate list.

For other students, career decisions have been made well before their senior year. For pre-meds, medical school will be the next step. For pre-law students, law school is probably on the horizon. There are still choices to be made about schools and programs, but those choices are relatively few and relatively clear.

But for too many students, even at the beginning of the senior year, their career plans may be no more specific than to graduate and look for a job. If that is the case for you, then you are at risk of just drifting on into and through life. If that's the way you want to live, that's your choice. But if you do want to take control of your life after college, there are two books which you absolutely must have—not online and not on your Kindle and not on your tablet, but real paper and print books!

The two books you must have are *What Color is your Parachute?* by Richard Bolles and *If You Don't Know Where You are Going, You'll Probably End Up Somewhere Else* by David Campbell.

What Color is your Parachute? is, according to Amazon.com, "the world's most popular job-hunting guide with more than ten million copies sold." This book will walk you through a structured job seeking process, while at the same time providing you with numerous tips for resumes, cover letters and job interviews. Be careful, however, to buy the most recent version of this book. *Parachute* is published in a new edition each year, and the year of that version is always included in the title. Each edition is updated with the newest information about the job market, so don't try to save a few dollars by getting a copy two or three years old, since in the fast changing economy we live in, that information will certainly be out of date.

The second book, *If You Don't Know Where You are Going, You'll Probably End Up Somewhere Else*, is written by one of the two developers of the "Strong Interest Inventory" and should be used in relation to your results from that question-naire.

Special tip: If you are facing any career uncertainty at the beginning of your senior year and you haven't taken the "Strong Interest Inventory" by now, you have no choice: take it! The results of this inventory can be one of the most crucial pieces of information you can possibly have at this point in your life.

Secret 18

Study Abroad

"When you come to a fork in the road, take it."

—Yogi Berra

We live in a global economy, and globalization has become a fact of life. Yet the United States, certainly one of the most important players on the global stage, is becoming more and more insular and parochial. Currently, only about 46% of Americans hold a valid passport. More interesting, however, is that there is an almost perfect match between those states that voted for Romney in 2012 and those states with the lowest percentage of passport holders, while those states that voted for Obama have the highest percentage of passport holders.

Specifically, according to a recent study, "the top 18 states with the highest percentage of passport holders (states where at least 44% of the population has passports) all had a majority of their population vote for Obama in 2012 (Alaska the sole exception). Alternately, the bottom 12 states all had a majority of their population vote for Romney." (Source: www.theexpeditioner.com, "How many Americans have a passport?"). As is so much the case in modern America, we have really become two nations, one in the mid-west and south that is increasingly inward and xenophobic, the other on the two coasts, looking outward to the wider world.

Which group would you rather be in?

Assuming that you would like to be a part of the future of our world and not part of this country's isolated and frightened past, you must become a citizen of the world. To accomplish this, there are three things that you must do.

First, of course, if you don't already have one, get a passport. Even though right now you may not see yourself going abroad

---

any time soon, your passport will be valid for ten years, and you will absolutely be using it before then.

Second, study at least one modern foreign language in college, probably Spanish and, if possible, Chinese. And include in your studies not just the language, but the history and geography of South America, Europe and Asia. In a study conducted a few years ago among college age Americans, "63 percent could not find Iraq or Saudi Arabia on a map, and 75 percent could not point out Iran or Israel." Even more appallingly, "forty-four percent couldn't find any one of these four countries." (Source: www.cnn.com, "Study: Geography Greek to Young Americans"). If democracy depends on an educated electorate, I fear for the future of this country. But at least you can do your part to not let this dreary situation become any worse.

Third, travel and study abroad. Most colleges will have programs for study abroad, often linked to on-campus academic courses, programs, and majors. Go online to identify opportunities for summer, semester, and yearlong courses of study. Plan on going to a country that speaks the language you have been studying as a way of getting real world experience with that language (or if you are really into risk taking, go to a country where you can't speak a word of their language). But however you do it, make studying abroad an expected part of your college plans.

Special tip: Employers are desperate for college graduates who are bilingual. If you can speak, and even write, in a second language, your career options and possibilities expand exponentially.

Secret 19

Get a Mentor

" **A** mentor is someone who sees more talent and ability within you than you see in yourself and helps bring it out in you."

—Bob Proctor

Several years ago I was watching a Mafia-type action movie, and in this one scene the older gangster was taking his new protégé to meet some of the "wise guys" at a local Italian restaurant. As they were walking along the sidewalk on their way to the meeting, the older guy told his young colleague that he was going to introduce him as "a friend of mine." He explained that this introduction meant that the younger man was under his protection and guidance. He further explained that if he were to introduce his friend as "a friend of ours," it would mean that his protégé was a "made man," a sworn in member of the Cosa Nostra. (Later in the movie and after he had "made his bones," the young man, now a hardened criminal, was in fact introduced as "a friend of ours.")

Without forcing the analogy too much, these two kinds of introductions define the two kinds of mentors you will need to be successful in college and beyond.

The "you are a friend of mine" mentorship will be what is called your academic mentor. This will be one of your professors, probably in your academic major, who has taken a personal interest in you and your success in college. This is a relationship that you should cultivate carefully and intentionally (but do not be so pushy as to ask directly "will you be my mentor?"). Identify this person as soon as you can in your college career, although in most likelihood you will not settle on this person before your junior year, when you begin to focus in on a specific major or career path. Your academic mentor, who may well be your advisor or one of your major professors, can be of immense help to you during your college career and can help connect you to people outside of college.

The second kind of mentor you will need is of the "he's one of us" kind. This is a person who will be of greatest value to you after college, although as you develop your network during your junior and senior years, you may have already begun establishing a relationship with this person. Usually this person, let's call him or her your professional mentor, will be someone who works in your company or profession. In addition to providing you with help in your career development, this person can be very useful in guiding you through the sometimes Byzantine maze of company or professional politics and culture.

There is an important difference, however, between these two kinds of mentorships. The first—"he's a friend of mine"—is largely a one-way transaction. Other than the satisfaction that comes from helping another person, your academic mentor is largely on the giving end of the transaction, while you are on the receiving end.

The second kind of mentorship—"he's a friend of ours"—is generally much more reciprocal, in that you are bringing something to the relationship. As you develop this mentorship, please be aware of this distinction. Don't just ask yourself what this other person can do for you, ask as well what you can do for him or her.

Special tip: Although the temptation can sometimes be great, be very careful about developing a personal or even intimate relationship with your professional mentor. Such relationships do, of course, develop but more often than not lead to personal and professional trouble.

Secret 20

Document your Experiences

"What goes unseen counts for nothing."
—Robert Greene

You never know when something you have done, witnessed, written or produced will come in handy. Remember that if you have followed some of the suggestions I have made in this book, you will be applying for various scholarships, internships and, eventually, one or more jobs. Having ready at hand some kind of documentation of your experiences can make such applications much less painless.

How you will go about this documentation will of course be up to you. Some people find that blogging can help them keep an accurate record of their college experiences. Others, less comfortable with writing, find using a video recorder a useful way of recording important conversations and events.

Many people like to keep a diary or journal. Others like to make scrapbooks, either digital or traditional, to share with friends

---

and family and, properly edited, prospective employers.

Look for opportunities to get your name in print. Write a thought-provoking article for the campus newspaper. Pick a topic that you are passionate about and express your opinions on paper. Write letters to the editors of your campus, local and back home newspapers.

In whatever way you choose, be sure to keep copies or some other record of your work. If you can keep all of this material in one place, one file or one folder, all the better.

Special tip: Although this suggestion may seem a bit extreme, keep everything that you write or otherwise produce during your college career. You may find, for example, that a topic you began exploring in a paper for your freshman writing class will form the basis for a more developed research paper in one of your other classes, even a year or two later. And, of course, if your major is of the kind that will produce a portfolio, begin collecting that material on day one.

Secret 21

Network to grow
your Networth

"The most important single ingredient in the formula of success is knowing how to get along with people."
—Theodore Roosevelt

Although perhaps overly cynical, the old saying "It's not *what* you know, it's *who* you know" still rings true. Besides the friendships and personal relationships you can establish through networking, you will also be keeping up with your profession, developing your career and even landing your first, or a new, job. The thousands of jobs posted online receive hundreds of applications, yet some experts argue that the "invisible job market" accounts for as much as 80% of new hires. The only way you can access that invisible market is through networking.

Networking can be done online or face to face. You have probably begun your online networking through Facebook. Keep

---

your account up-to-date during your college career, but realize that Facebook is primarily a social, not a professional, network.

As soon as you can, and certainly no later than your junior year, establish an account on LinkedIn, which is to professional networking what Facebook is to social networking. Through LinkedIn, you will be able to follow various businesses and industries, participate in relevant group discussions and reach out to others in your field. You will also be able to use LinkedIn to access the networks of your college alumni and alumni associations. Remember that those who have graduated from your college or university have a real interest in helping other graduates.

To find out how to manage your professional networks properly, go over to my blog at richbefore30.com.

Start an interest group on social media is another great strategy for networking. If you are passionate about a particular cause or movement develop a group where people with similar interests can come together and meet. This strategy is great to develop both your social as well as professional network.

Face to face networking, however, provides the personal touch that internet networking does not. Attend networking events with professionals in your city. The relationships you build in these circles will give you access to present and future career opportunities. Once you make a new personal contact, be sure to follow up with a short email within a few days of meeting that person. For those contacts that you see as being of particular importance, keep the relationship alive with an email every few months. Let those important contacts know about the progress you're making in school, your internships and volunteer activities and even interesting class projects that you are working on.

Special tip: By no later than the beginning of your junior year, make up a set of business cards for yourself. With all of the desktop publishing and printing resources available to you, this can be done for almost no cost. Use the templates available to you online. Even use the logo of your school as long as you are still a legitimate student. Almost no students have business cards, so think of the impression you will make when you meet a new professional contact!

With these strategies you are more than prepared to go on your mission. Remember that success is not years away it begins today. Seize the moment!

DID YOU KNOW?

On Mission: 21 Secrets for College Success is a project of the non-profit organization: R.I.C.H Before 30 (RB3). RB3 was launched by Laptop Lifestyle, LLC which are both founded by Mwale Henry and Chantel Morant.

The RB3 movement is all about empowering 20-Somethings and Millennials to **R**eclaim their **I**ndependence and **C**reate **H**ope (RICH) for a better future.

We are a global network of young people who strive to positively impact the world through entrepreneurship and service.

While Coach Chantel is **H**elping **O**ther **P**eople **E**xcel, Coach Mwale is serving others in **F**inding their **A**bundant **I**ncrease **T**his **H**our.

F.A.I.T.H TOUR

Finding **A**bundant **I**ncrease **T**his **H**our

Coach Mwale is traveling to colleges, high schools, churches, and community centers throughout 6 countries sharing the message of F.A.I.T.H.

His new book, **The Power of Identity: 7 Steps to Overtake and Dominate** draws upon Coach Mwale's vast personal experience, spirituality and a liberal dose of common sense as he provides a foundational guide for personal development.

Writing in a lively and easily relatable style, he touches on issues ranging from how to deal with criticism, fear of failure to overcoming the fear of rejection. His message is simple yet compelling: attitude is everything and ultimately you are in charge of your own destiny!

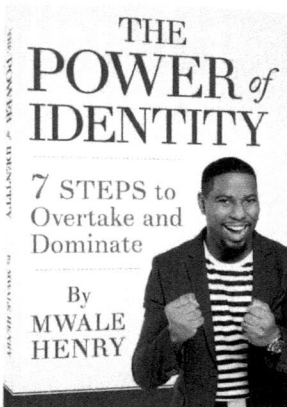

Get your copy at www.CoachMwale.com

Claim your FREE gift at www.StartTheMission.org

MISSION OF H.O.P.E. TOUR

Helping **O**ther **P**eople Excel

Coach Chantel has embarked upon a 20-city Mission of H.O.P.E. Tour, to help high school juniors, seniors and college freshman, make college count!

On a Mission: 21 Secrets for College Success lays out easy-to-follow strategies for first-time college students to understand the right things to focus on to get better grades, stand-out from the competition while enjoying the best 4 years of their life!

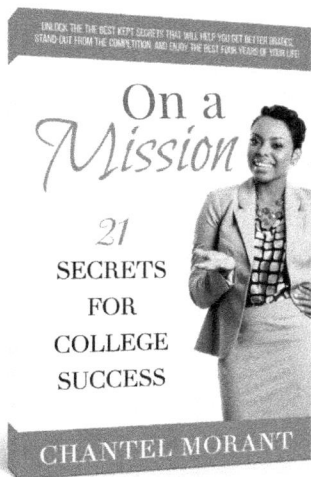

**Get your copy at
www.ChantelMorant.com**

ABOUT THE AUTHOR

MISSION OF H.O.P.E. TOUR

Helping Other People Excel

OVERVIEW

This year, Coach Chantel will embark upon an international tour to inspire millennials to achieve their dreams. There has never been a more urgent time than now to help young people counteract the negative influences that bombard them on a daily bases. Realizing this fact, the Mission of H.O.P.E. tour is designed to expose high school juniors, seniors and college freshman, to the possibilities that exist when vision meets determination and one is prepared to seize an opportunity.

WHO IS COACH CHANTEL?

Coach Chantel is one of the most highly requested millennial speakers for conferences and educational institutions throughout the world. At 25 years old, Chantel became one of the youngest faculty members to teach at her undergraduate university as an adjunct-professor. Her goal is to be a living example to young people of what is possible with clear vision and focus.

True to her calling, Chantel has made it a personal mission to travel the world to inspire young adults to maximize their potential and live the life of their dreams! She made an early decision in life to secure a positive future through education.

While earning both a bachelors and masters degree, Coach Chantel traveled to more than 11 countries by age 22. She quickly realized that true knowledge did not end in the classroom, but that it must be present in every facet of life and bear active and evolving fruit at every stage.

Today Coach Chantel is an author, international speaker and business coach. As a coach she teaches thousands of entrepreneurs how to grow their business with digital technology. Her client portfolio generates in excess of $50,000 in revenue each month. She personally commands a team of more than1200 entrepreneurs domestically and abroad.

From the boardroom to the classroom, Chantel's moniker "Coach" represents her leadership style well: always positive and committed to success.

ABOUT THE BOOK

On a Mission: 21 Secrets For College Success is the ultimate guide for students who seek the competitive edge. This book is filled with **ready-to-use strategies** that take the complexity from the college experience, by exploring key habits that will make the **difference between success and failure**.

The transition from high school to college is often the biggest challenge for students. **Approximately 30%** of first year college students **either drop out or do not return** to the same school for their second year. Many factors contribute to this. The end result is that **only 60% of college freshmen** graduate within 6 years (Brigdgeedu.com, 2015).

As an author and speaker, Coach Chantel seeks to equip students with the necessary strategies to overcome obstacles so that they have maximum success during school.

TOPICS

On a Mission: 21 Secrets For College Success is divided into three sections:

Your Academic Life, Your Campus Life and Your Life After College.

Topics include:

- Developing good study habits
- Improving writing skills
- Money management
- Study abroad
- Career planning

**Essential Read For High School Juniors,
Seniors & College Freshman!**

SPEAKING TOPICS & WORKSHOP

21 Secrets For College Success

Chantel will help students develop best practices for implementing the success secrets, through candid commentary and interaction. Audience participation is highly encouraged so that students leave with an actionable game-plan to overcome their toughest challenges.

Social Media Etiquette

The saying: "What goes unseen counts for nothing," has never been more true than in today's society. Chantel sheds light on social media etiquette, relationship building and the most underutilized strategies for building a bankable brand at every stage of life.

Transforming the Impossible into I'm-Possible

It was difficult for most to predict that a poor girl from the heart of Baltimore City, would be anything besides a statistic. Despite all odds, Chantel rose from her mediocre beginning and took charge of her destiny.

By 22 years old Chantel traveled to more than 12 countries, dined with princes and presidents, became an entrepreneur, author and recognized leader within the digital marketing industry.

Get Rid of Stinking Thinking

A positive mind translates to a positive life. Thoughts are like seeds if you plant a rotten seed your crops will not grow! Having a positive mental attitude is one of the main factors of Chantel's success.

During this conversation, she gives poignant stories and key strategies for audiences to eliminate their negative mindset and enjoy a more vibrant life.

PREVIOUS ENGAGEMENTS

Central Scholarship AMERICAN UNIVERSITY CLARK ATLANTA UNIVERSITY BLACK COLLEGE EXPO LINCOLN COLLEGE OF TECHNOLOGY AIPAC

NOW BOOKING

"Social Media Etiquette Workshop: Pics, Posts & Problems."
January, 2015 Clark Atlanta University

Coach Chantel delivers...

Keynote addresses and workshops at non profit organizations, high schools and colleges around the world including:

- Baltimore City College
- Central Scholarship Bureau
- American Israel Public Affairs Committee
- Clark Atlanta University
- American University

"Chantel's presentation style is **engaging, energetic and packed with information**. As a speaker, she touches the intellect as well as the heart. In short, **her message is mandatory** for those students who are serious about success!"
—Dennis Kimbro, The Wealth Choice

BOOK NOW!

Claim your FREE gift at www.StartTheMission.org

MORE ABOUT COACH CHANTEL

Chantel Morant is the consummate scholar, in fact she has loved education her whole life. The night before her first day of school she fell asleep with a backpack on. Always equipped for the journey ahead, Chantel gives truth to the statement: when preparation meets opportunity, the rest is history.

A native of Baltimore, Maryland Chantel matriculated through the public school system where she received a high school diploma from Baltimore City College, a National Blue Ribbon School of Excellence.

She went on to receive a B.A. in Mass Media Arts from Clark Atlanta University. Three months after graduating, Chantel packed her bags and embarked upon a solo mission to Johannesburg, South Africa. While serving as the Communications Director for the Ubuntu Institute, Chantel learned the indelible imprint Nelson Mandela had on the country. The sight of cooperation amongst past adversaries amid the glaring economic stratification, fueled Chantel's desire to seek higher learning in international affairs. In 2011, she was selected among thousands of applicants to receive a full academic scholarship to American University in Washington, D.C.

Today Chantel resides in Atlanta, Georgia and lives what she calls the Laptop Lifestyle. As a digital marketing strategist, Chantel teaches professionals how to elevate their brand online.

Chantel believes that the information age affords previously disadvantage communities the opportunity to close the income gap. She is the co-founder of R.I.C.H. Before 30 (RB3) a movement designed to empower young people to **R**eclaim **I**ndependence and **C**reate **H**ope for the future. RB3 now has a presence on 5 continents and its membership is growing with young social entrepreneurs striving to make a positive impact on the world.

BOOK NOW!

Contact: Coach Chantel
Phone: 410.330.5432
Web: www.ChantelMorant.com
Gmail: yourcoachchantel@gmail.com